SCARBOROUGH
IN OLD PHOTOGRAPHS

CASTLE HILL, the harbour with both sail and steam fishing boats, and a small boy on the quayside: a typical photograph of early Scarborough.

Front Cover Illustration:

THREE FISHER GIRLS spend a rare moment of leisure knitting stockings. They are sitting on herring barrels on the quay and something in the harbour has caught their attention.

SCARBOROUGH
IN OLD PHOTOGRAPHS

COLLECTED BY
DENIS COGGINS

ALAN SUTTON

Alan Sutton Publishing Limited
Phoenix Mill · Far Thrupp · Stroud · Gloucestershire

First published 1991

British Library Cataloguing in Publication Data

Around Scarborough in old photographs.
I. Coggins, D.
942.847

ISBN 0-86299-932-4

Typeset in 9/10 Korinna.
Typesetting and origination by
Alan Sutton Publishing Limited.
Printed in Great Britain by
The Bath Press, Avon.

CONTENTS

PACKING HERRINGS. For much of its thousand years of history the prosperity of Scarborough has depended largely on its fishing industry.

INTRODUCTION

Arthur Rowntree prefaced his 1930 *History of Scarborough* with a quotation from Cicero: 'Not to know what was done in the world before we were born is to remain forever a child.' There can be few people who live in Scarborough or visit the town who are not interested in its history. 'What was it like to live then?' is a question which fascinates us all.

It is of course only the last 130 years of the town's history which can be illustrated by photographs, but for these years to be placed in their proper perspective it is necessary to have some idea of what had happened previously and of the geographical features which have shaped the development of Scarborough. Two of these features have been of paramount importance: the Castle Hill provided a site which was an unrivalled observation post and could be easily defended, while the South Bay was for all practical purposes the only harbour between the Tyne and the Humber.

People have been living in the Scarborough area for many thousands of years – perhaps the best-known mesolithic site in England is that which was found at Star Carr near Seamer – and finds have been made which represent all the major phases of the long prehistoric period culminating in the arrival of the Romans who established a signal station on Castle Hill. But 'Scarborough' as the name of a distinctive settlement only appears much later. It almost certainly commemorated the nickname 'Skarthi', meaning 'hare-lip', given to a Viking named Thorgils who, with his brother Kormak, was raiding in England around AD 960 and who seems to have founded the town. It must have been only a small settlement and it was not until the middle of the twelfth century that Scarborough began to grow beneath the protective walls of the castle newly built by William le Gros. The new town was then granted a charter by King Henry II. A hundred years later Scarborough was expanding outside its original boundary ditch and wall so that the burgesses were given the neighbouring manor of Falsgrave to help ease the pressure of an increasing population. By about 1300, according to Rowntree, '... probably no small town had reached a higher state of privilege and independence than Scarborough ...'

This prosperity did not continue, however, and for the next 350 years the fortunes of the town varied greatly: fluctuations in trade, quarrels between town and castle, plague, piracy, smuggling, and attacks by Scots, French and Dutch during foreign wars all led to many changes in prosperity, but the net result seems to have been a gradual decline in the status and commercial importance of Scarborough. During all this time, too, a constant source of worry and expense was the upkeep of the harbour and its quays. There was frequent damage by storms and the town was often hard put to it to find money for essential repairs, much less for desirable improvements. As well as local efforts to raise money there were frequent appeals – not always successful – to central government. The traumatic effects of the Civil War were felt in Scarborough to perhaps a rather greater degree than most other towns, for the castle was twice besieged and the tower partly destroyed by bombardment.

Just before the Civil War, however, a discovery had been made which was to change the pattern of future development of the town: the Spa (or Spaw) waters with their medicinal properties. By the end of the seventeenth century 'taking the waters' had become fashionable, and as travel became somewhat easier in the next century more and more people visited the town, especially during the summer. Early in the nineteenth century it became apparent to many that the future of the town was to lie with its role as a resort rather than a port, and both individuals and the Corporation began schemes of improvement for the benefit of visitors. The arrival of the railway from York in 1875 led to a surge in visitor numbers – including for the first time the less well-off – and in growth. Between 1841 and 1861 the population of Scarborough almost doubled, from under 10,000 to over 17,000.

It is from this time on that, increasingly, the important events and changes in the life of Scarborough were recorded by photographers. Few of the early photographs survive and they are of course the more valuable for that. By the early years of this century photography had become commonplace and it was becoming practicable for the ordinary person to take pictures of his family, friends and home. Visitors to the town wanted souvenir photographs of their holiday and the production of postcard views had become an important business.

There was much to record in Scarborough. Between 1861 and 1891 the population again doubled as did the number of occupied houses. Though shipbuilding ended about 1860 and overseas trade was in sharp decline fishing remained an important industry and improvements continued to be made to the harbour and its facilities. Tourism continued to expand. To cater for existing visitors and to attract more, constant improvements to the amenities of the town were made by private companies and especially by the Corporation: North Bay rock gardens, Valley Bridge, South Cliff tramway, the Aquarium, Marine Drive, Alexandra Gardens, Floral Hall, Peasholm Park, to name but a few of an impressive list. These were imaginative and largely successful, if costly, projects which helped to project the image of Scarborough as 'the Queen of Watering Places'.

The trauma of the First World War, when Scarborough found itself unexpectedly in the front line, was succeeded by the problems of the recession which accompanied peace. Visitors continued to arrive, however, many of them by the increasingly popular motor-bus, and on the whole Scarborough continued to grow and to prosper through the 1920s and '30s.

In 1938 the Corporation produced a report on desirable future developments and identified four main groups of visitors for whose needs it would be necessary to cater. The wealthier classes would require good hotels, high-class entertainments, orderly and dignified surroundings and good shops. It was hoped to persuade many of the wealthy to spend their winters in the town or to retire there. The well-to-do weekend visitor arriving by train or car needed a good and attractive hotel, a convenient garage, facilities for sports and a variety of amusements, especially some novelty not found elsewhere. The middle-class visitor and his family came to enjoy the sea and the sands. They required cheap and comfortable lodgings and organized entertainment. The day excursionist and the poorer family arrived by rail or bus. Their chief requirements were the sea and sands, fun-fair, skating rink, dance-hall and cheap good refreshments. Having identified the customers, the areas of the town appropriate to each group and the problems involved, the Corporation proceeded to plan for a future which looked bright. Plans were certainly needed: on August Bank Holiday Saturday, 1939 no less than 102 trains arrived in Scarborough station. Only a month later, however, the outbreak of war put a temporary stop to any thoughts of further development.

When, in 1798, long before the invention of photography, Thomas Hinderwell wrote his *History of Scarborough* he stated '. . . the object of this Work is to exhibit a topographic and economic view of Scarborough . . . and to rescue from obscurity the remains of information relative to its Antiquities . . .' This book in its own small way attempts in turn 'to rescue from obscurity' some images of a Scarborough which is gone, or rather images of a changing Scarborough recorded by photographers, most of them anonymous amateurs who took pictures of friends, places and events, and the myriad other things which interested them. Looking at these photographs helps us to appreciate what G.M. Trevelyan called '. . . the quasi-miraculous fact that once on this earth . . . walked other men and women, as actual as we are today . . . thinking their own thoughts, swayed by their own passions . . . but now all gone . . .'

SECTION ONE

The Borough

HISTORY AND GROWTH

SCARBOROUGH CASTLE from the north. Built by William le Gros in the twelfth century on a headland protected on the seaward side by steep cliffs, the Castle remained impregnable for hundreds of years. During the Civil War, however, it was besieged and, though it held out for months, was finally forced to yield. In 1645 it was subjected to such heavy bombardment that '... in 3 dayes the great Tower splitt in two and that side which was battered fell to the ground ...' It was never repaired.

THE ATTACK ON SCARBOROUGH by Harald Hardrada is recreated during an historical pageant performed in the Castle in 1912, which portrayed episodes from the history of the town. The real attack took place in the autumn of 1066 when Harald, King of Norway, joined forces with Tostig, the disaffected brother of King Harold of England, and raided along the east coast before attacking York where they were defeated.

ANOTHER SCENE FROM THE PAGEANT: sword dancers performing before King Richard III. In his *History of Scarborough* Thomas Hinderwell wrote, '. . . the Duke of Gloucester obtained the royal dignity by treachery and established it in blood. After his coronation in 1483 he proceeded to York for the purpose of a second inauguration and of ingratiating himself with his subjects. He also visited Scarborough with Anne his queen and resided some time in the Castle . . .' Hinderwell's view of the character of Richard III would not meet with general agreement today.

SCARBOROUGH CASTLE played an important part in the Civil War. Sir Hugh Cholmley, though MP for the town and at first a supporter of Parliament, later declared for the king and defended the castle for a year against many determined attacks. His wife, portrayed here in the pageant, remained at the castle throughout where she ' . . . endured much hardship . . . and in the greatest danger would never be daunted . . . she did not omit to visit the sick and take extraordinary care of them.'

GEORGE FOX of the Society of Friends (Quakers) was one of the more famous men to have been imprisoned in Scarborough Castle, sent there in 1665 because of his religious principles. Hinderwell says ' . . . the exemplary patience, great humility and inoffensive conduct of George Fox so conciliated the esteem of the governor and officers . . . that they became his friends . . .' He was released by order of the king on 1 September 1666. Here, the notice of his release is being read to him.

THE DECLARATION OF INDULGENCE, issued by James II in 1688, suspended laws against Catholics and Nonconformists. All clergymen were supposed to read out this Declaration in church; the vicar of Scarborough refused to do so and was taken to task for this by the mayor. When the mayor refused to apologize for actually striking the vicar he was seized by soldiers stationed in the castle and tossed in a blanket. One hopes that Scarborough has become more tolerant since then.

ONE OF THE FIRST BUILDINGS to be developed as the town of Scarborough began to grow under the protection of the Castle was the parish church, St Mary's, seen here at the top of Church Stairs Street. Parts of the fabric of the church date from the late twelfth century and it remained the only parish church until the beginning of the nineteenth century.

TWO SOLDIERS IN THE CASTLE YARD, C. 1880. The barrack buildings behind them originated in the panic which followed the Jacobite rising of 1745. Hasty measures for the defence of the town were taken in the face of a possible attack by the Scots which in fact never materialized.

PART OF WALKER'S SHIPYARDS in 1895. Note the two cannon being used as counterweights on the crane. Perhaps these too were relics of the 1745 scare when many cannon were mounted for the defence of the harbour.

THREE VIEWS OF SCARBOROUGH taken from an album which was one of a series of town views published by Charles Reynolds and Co. and printed in Germany. They show the South Bay, Spa Bridge and North Bay as they were at about the end of the nineteenth century.

THEY ARE NOT PHOTOGRAPHS but engravings made from photographs. This can be seen clearly by comparing the engraving of the North Bay (top of page 15) with the photograph (below). The latter is not dated but it shows the new sea-wall, begun in 1887, partly completed, while the pavilion at the seaward end of the pier, built after 1881, is not shown.

ANOTHER ENGRAVING from the same album showing Scarborough as seen from Oliver's Mount.

THE OLD BAR proudly displaying the royal arms and a variety of other decorations, possibly in honour of a visit to the town by the Prince of Wales.

ST NICHOLAS HOUSE on St Nicholas Cliff was owned Mr J.W. Woodall, a banker and a man of great ability and many interests. He was particularly known for his pioneering work on the possibilities of breeding and farming sea fish. In 1903, after Mr Woodhall's death, the house was acquired by the Corporation for use as the Town Hall.

THE PAGODA. In complete contrast, but still very much an important Scarborough building, is this pagoda in Peasholm Park seen here floodlit shortly after its construction.

THE OLD TOWN of Scarborough had lots of steep and narrow streets, many of which have since been 'developed'. This photograph shows another view of Church Stairs Street (seen on page 12) with St Mary's Place on the right. Notice the open gutters down each side of the street with steps across them.

A WONDERFULLY ATMOSPHERIC PICTURE of a solitary figure in a wet and deserted Cross Street of the 1920s. The next two photographs show some dramatic changes to this street.

CROSS STREET, taken in 1936, before and during demolition work prior to rebuilding.

ANOTHER OF SCARBOROUGH'S OLD STREETS, again with a solitary walker and again undated but probably in the 1920s. This is St Mary's Street and the corner of Low Conduit Street. The Leeds Arms and the chemists shop of Longden and Ghallentree are visible.

QUAY STREET is often spelt 'Key' on old maps and documents. It was one of the most important streets of the old town, running parallel to the foreshore. During the eighteenth century it held the Town Hall, which in the later nineteenth century was converted into a Methodist chapel. The house on the left was occupied in the 1930s by Mr Edwards, a diver employed by the Harbour Commissioners.

THE IVY HOUSE on Sandside with the battery, another of the defensive works built to counter the '45 rebellion, behind it on Castle Hill.

POTTER LANE, a little street which was largely destroyed by a land-mine in 1941. The houses were rebuilt and it is now called Castle Gardens.

CHURCH STAIRS STREET. This beautiful photograph, taken from the top of the street, seems to capture the character and atmosphere of the old town. It was probably taken in around 1890.

SCALBY ROAD. The visitor arriving in Scarborough along the road from Whitby today would hardly recognize the corner of Scalby Road seen in these two photographs, *c.* 1930. Nor would he be able to see *Charlie Chan* at the Capitol, *Twelve Good Men* at the Londesborough or *Two in a Crowd* at the Futurist.

THE SCALBY MILLS HOTEL beside Scalby Beck was one of Scarborough's many inns and hotels. This photograph was taken in 1897 and is the first of a half-dozen showing some of the old town's hostelries.

THE STRAWBERRY GARDENS INN was once one of the most popular locals on the outskirts of the town. The building shown here – probably in the 1890s – is still standing, forming part of the disused Snowdrift Laundry in Scalby Road.

THE BEEHIVE INN on Sandside next door to the Sandside post office, again probably about the turn of the century. Its sign used to read:

For in this house we're all alive
Good beer will make you funny
If you are dry as you pass by
Come in and taste our honey.

THE LANCASTER INN with (presumably) the landlord Mr Raper and his family at the door. J. Raper is listed as landlord in the *Scarborough Directory* of 1893.

ANOTHER WELL-KNOWN INN of the old town was the Three Mariners. Its sign of a ship's figurehead can just be seen in the photograph of the Marine Stores on page 35.

THE TALBOT HOTEL in Queen Street with the staff outside the front door. Presumably the cab also belonged to the hotel. The sign advertises a Market Dinner for 1s. 6d.

THE WESTFIELD HOTEL, unlike the Talbot Hotel which remains little changed in appearance, was one of the many buildings demolished in 1936 to make way for the Odeon cinema. A note on the reverse of the original photograph says this was previously the home of Dr C. Rooke, a well-known doctor and geologist who in the 1860s published his anti-establishment medical paper *The Anti-Lancet.*

SITE CLEARANCE in preparation for the building of the Odeon, 1936.

ROWNTREE'S OLD TYME CAFÉ, perhaps the best-known and most frequented café in Scarborough, seen here after being damaged in the bombardment of 1914.

THE END OF SPREAD EAGLE LANE with a coal depot on the right of the picture. The café sign which can be seen in the centre was for an establishment called The British Workman. This was probably one of a number of cafés of the same name started in the 1870s as non-alcoholic pubs. As well as serving drinks they provided entertainment and education, their 'penny readings' being especially popular.

THE SCARBOROUGH HOSPITAL had its beginnings in 1851 when a private meeting of better-off citizens decided to find money for a dispensary for the sick poor of the town. In 1858 a site was purchased in Elders Street and a building erected (upper picture). In succeeding years beds were installed and the charity became the Scarborough Dispensary and Accident Hospital. By 1891 the premises were seen to be far too small and a new site at Friars Entry was found. The new hospital (lower picture) was opened in 1893 and remained the town's hospital until 1934.

THE OLD BAR viewed from Westbrough. Though apparently medieval, the Old Bar was in fact a late product of the Gothic Revival in architecture, being built in 1850. It was demolished in 1890 because of the obstruction which it caused to traffic.

THE WINDMILL IN MILL STREET is Scarborough's last surviving mill. In the early nineteenth century the town boasted at least four. This very fine photograph shows the mill as it was about 1890.

A VIEW OF THE BACK of the quaintly – or aptly – named Paradise, taken from the Castle Dykes. The atmosphere of calm which pervades this fine picture is in contrast to the bustle of the harbour or the throngs of visitors only a short distance away.

A PHOTOGRAPHER'S ADVERTISING CARD Mr Moxell was one of many commercial photographers in the town in the 1880s.

A SMALL GENERAL SHOP with a girl waiting outside – an undated but undoubtedly early photograph. The exact location is uncertain but there must have been many small shops of this type in Scarborough.

ANOTHER LITTLE SHOP with a girl outside. This time the street name – Longwestgate – has fortunately been included in the picture. The shop was on the corner with Castlegate and its rather fine bowed windows were later acquired by the Castle Museum at York.

A FRUIT AND VEGETABLE STALL at a street market probably in or near St Helens Square. As well as shops old Scarborough had many markets, on Newborough, St Nicholas Street and St Thomas Street. Though a large market hall was purpose-built in the 1850s, the old street markets did not disappear.

JOHN JACKSON'S DRAPERS SHOP in Queen Street with its window display of summer hats and its sign of a huge shirt – or is it a smock? Mr Jackson came to Scarborough as a pauper and ended as mayor.

SIMON PURNELL AND SON. As would be expected, Scarborough had several marine stores like Purnell's on Sandside. Down the alley in the centre of the picture it is just possible to see the sign – a ship's figurehead – of the Three Mariners inn.

A HAY AND STRAW MERCHANT'S STORE is perhaps at first sight unexpected in a maritime town. It is easy to forget, however, how many horses were in use before the days of the motor car and how expensive it was to find food for them in a town. In the 1890s – about the time of this picture – there were at least nine livery stables in Scarborough, including Foxton's own at the Grand Hotel.

THERE WERE TWO MAJOR BREWERIES in Scarborough – Nesfields and the Scarborough and Whitby. The drays in this yard bear the name of G. & H. Hudson.

TWO OF SCARBOROUGH'S PRINCIPAL STREETS: Eastborough (above) and Newborough (below). The lower photograph was taken in 1906 and shows the tramlines installed in 1904. The upper photograph is not dated but is likely to be a few years earlier.

HEPWORTHS, on the corner of Queen Street and Market Street, about 1880.

THE SAME PREMISES in about 1901, after it had been acquired by William Boyes and extended. The development of this firm is representative of the way Scarborough's overall growth and prosperity has been reflected in its shopping streets.

WILLIAM BOYES'S STORE in Market Street, *c.* 1890, with staff outside the door. William, a Scarborough man, founded his business on buying manufacturers' remnants cheaply and retailing them, also cheaply. His store was known affectionately as 'The Rem'.

THE DRAPERY DEPARTMENT of 'The Rem' in the early years of the century.

THE HOUSEHOLD GOODS DEPARTMENT.

THE INCREDIBLE 'ORIENTAL BAZAAR'.

SCARBOROUGH STATION BUILDING with its well-known clock tower. This was erected in 1884 and this photograph seems to have been taken very soon after that date (compare the picture on page 43). The York to Scarborough line was opened on 7 July 1845 and within a month of that date the first excursion train arrived from Newcastle. The railway had a tremendous effect on the growth of Scarborough's popularity and by 1900 over 300,000 passengers per year were using the station.

AFTER ARRIVING AT THE STATION BY TRAIN visitors were dependent upon horse-drawn carriages for local journeys. Even in 1919, when this photograph was taken, motor vehicles were extremely rare.

A VERY SMART EQUIPAGE in the yard of the Grand Hotel stables, with two prospective passengers on the stairs. In the 1890s Scarborough had at least nine livery stables, an indication of the fact that, until the arrival of the motor car, the horse reigned supreme.

A CABMEN'S SHELTER, taken in 1898. As well as equipages such as that seen above, there were of course many cabs plying for hire. There was usually no shelter for the driver on his vehicle so most towns provided buildings like this one.

SCARBOROUGH STATION with the Pavilion Hotel in the background, and to the left the Brunswick Hotel. A row of cabs is waiting in the street beside the small cabmen's shelter. Note that the photograph was taken before the tramlines had been laid but after the enclosing railings had been installed (compare page 41).

SCARBOROUGH GOODS STATION was opened in 1902 and this photograph, taken only a few years later, shows the team of carthorses, most of them greys, needed for deliveries.

THE SOUTH CLIFF TRAMWAY was opened in 1875 and is shown in this very damaged early photograph. The Queens Parade tramway opened in 1878 but was closed nine years later. The Central tramway opened in 1881, the St Nicholas in 1929 and the North Cliff in 1930.

ELECTRIC TRAMLINES being laid over the top of the Aquarium. By 1904 Scarborough had an electric street tram system using twenty-eight cars on five miles of 3 ft 6 in gauge track forming two circular routes.

TRAM AND BUSES on the foreshore road. At first the trams were owned by the Scarborough Tramways Co., which in 1911 was fined 10s. for every day it failed to provide a service. The company was later acquired by the Corporation, and in 1931 trams were replaced by a bus service.

THE ODEON ROUNDABOUT as it was in the 1920s with both trams and buses very much in evidence. The charabanc in the foreground offers trips to Oliver's Mount.

A FINE EARLY DAIMLER complete with carbide lamps, AA badge and monkey mascot. The driver, in uniform, started his taxi business on leaving the army.

THE FORD MODEL T in its van form was the standby of most delivery firms. The driver and his mate in this photograph were Billy Latter and Jack Bowes, taken in the 1920s, a little later than the Daimler shown above.

THIS BOYES STORES VAN driven by Mr B. Raper is bigger and better than its predecessor on page 47. By the 1930s, vehicles on the whole were beginning to be rather more refined and also much more common.

NOT ALL EARLY MOTORING WAS FOR BUSINESS. The pleasure tour had started even before the First World War, though this photograph dates from the early 1920s. Charabancs such as this were supposed to be limited to 12 m.p.h.

COUNCILLOR PIRIE, mayor of Scarborough, 1897–8. Scarborough's long tradition of local government goes back to the twelfth century when the town was first granted a charter. In modern times the council has always been deeply involved in developing the town's amenities as well as in the mundane business of local government. Many of its mayors have been unusually farsighted and public-spirited men.

WILLIAM BOYES, mayor in 1924.

THE FALSGRAVE INFANTS' SCHOOL soon after opening. Education has always been one of the more important concerns of local government. Though the first so-called Lancasterian school was opened in 1864, it was not until 1873 that the Falsgrave Infants' School, the first of the new Board Schools, was opened in the borough. Note that the door is closed so it cannot be during school hours. The three children – who can hardly be described as 'infants' – look remarkably cheerful.

A GROUP OF ATTENDANTS outside the door of the South Baths in 1924.

TWO MORE ESSENTIAL SERVICES. Above we see the Scarborough police force assembled in the fire station yard. The date is uncertain but probably about the same as that of the lower photograph which shows the fire brigade with their first motor appliances, presented to them in 1913 by Mr G. Barnes.

SCARBOROUGH CORPORATION'S CATERING DEPARTMENT was highly regarded in the 1930s, as befits such an important seaside resort. Here staff are demonstrating their skills at a meal for the mayor and mayoress in the Town Hall.

A GROUP OF UNEMPLOYED MEN with toys which they had made for the Christmas trade at the Claremont Occupational Centre. Unemployment was high in Scarborough between the wars.

SECTION TWO

The Resort

THE SPA

THE SPA BRIDGE, a photograph taken from a postcard sent in 1922. Though the properties of the Spa waters were discovered in the early seventeenth century access to it was difficult. As more and more people came to 'take the waters', it became imperative to improve access from the town. The Spa Bridge was opened in 1827 as a toll bridge. It was bought by the Corporation and freed from toll in 1951.

DESIGNED BY SIR JOSEPH PAXTON, who also remodelled the grounds, this building replaced the first real public building at the Spa in 1856. The latter was the so-called Gothic Saloon designed by the well-known architect Wyatt in 1839. This is a lovely early photograph of a beach deserted except for a lady investigating the rock pools. Her perambulator – if that is what it is – stands abandoned on the beach behind her.

THE 'SALOON' OF PAXTON'S SPA was destroyed by fire in 1876 but was soon replaced by the much larger building seen in this photograph. Again we have a nearly deserted beach. Walshaw's bathing machines are being dragged up beyond the high tide mark. The only visitors to be seen are a lady – with umbrella – three children and a dog. Two of the children are moving too quickly for the camera to catch them, probably trying to keep warm on a typical English summer day.

THE PROMENADE AND SOUTH ROTUNDA OF THE SPA. The photograph must have been taken between 1867, when the Grand Hotel, seen right centre, was opened, and 1876, when the Spa saloon burnt down.

A FORMALLY DRESSED GROUP which may well be the resident orchestra, conducted by Herr Lutz for some years around 1890. The Spa was noted for its concerts which were provided by visiting orchestras as well as the resident orchestra. The building is the new Spa Hall, opened in 1880.

A LOVELY PHOTOGRAPH which perhaps sums up what Scarborough and the Spa meant to the late Victorians and Edwardians.

THE AUTHOR AND HIS MOTHER on the beach, c. 1927.

SCARBOROUGH BEACH. While the Spa may have been the centre of activity for some visitors, for most and especially for generations of children Scarborough was the beach and sand castles.

A FAMILY HOLIDAY PERHAPS. We can't quite make out what this party is doing except that it involves sand and water, buckets and spades, and of course a deckchair.

A HIGHLY ADVENTUROUS GROUP for whom the sand isn't important but the water is.

THE SOUTH BAY with the tide a long way out. In the foreground (left) is the entrance gate to the Spa. There is a long row of the cumbersome bathing machines essential for privacy when changing clothes. This is a very early photograph taken before the building of the foreshore road in 1877 or the Grand Hotel in 1867.

A GROUP OF BATHING MACHINES on the South Sands. The prospective bather entered the machine while it was on the beach. It was then drawn out into the sea by the horse so that the bather – having changed costumes in seclusion – could enter the sea with decorum.

A PROSPECTIVE BOAT TRIP – another essential part of the seaside holiday. 'There are,' said the author of Theakston's *Guide to Scarborough* (1880), 'few modes of recreation more romantic and enjoyable than a sail or a pull or a steam out to sea, especially to those who have never before trusted themselves on the treacherous ocean . . .' But first you have to get into the boat – which seems to have presented no problem for these children.

A BOARDING AID for the not so adventurous passenger, for whom embarking was more difficult. Ward Lock's *Guide* of 1911 described the solution: 'When the tide is out persons are conveyed to and from the boats on a kind of trolley or plank on wheels. This exhilarating ride is not included in the fare: the trolleyman is usually paid a penny a head . . .'

A RIDE ON THE TROLLEY may have been exhilarating for the passengers but it looks hard work for the trolleymen.

THE THREE LADIES pictured here, staying safely on the beach, don't look much like prospective sailors – or donkey riders either. The building behind them is the royal Northern Sea-Bathing Infirmary, later St Thomas's Hospital.

TWO PATIENT DONKEYS with their perhaps not so patient owner waiting for customers. The donkeys will probably be quite happy if no one turns up. The near one has a sort of box seat for a small child instead of a saddle.

ANOTHER GROUP OF DONKEYS with a different proprietor. In the background are the sea-water baths in a building which later became Corrigans Amusement Arcade.

NOT DONKEYS THIS TIME but a young entrepreneur with his goat-drawn dog-cart on the Spa slipway. He would take children for rides along the sands.

A BUSY DAY on the beach. Practically all the beach activities can be seen going on here in this turn-of-the-century holiday photograph.

THE SOUTH BAY AND HARBOUR during the holiday season before the First World War. The tide is in and so are the pleasure cobles, while most of the bathing machines are out.

WILL RICKETTS, a well-known Scarborough photographer, at work on the beach. One of the most important seaside institutions is shown in this charming picture of the beach photographer at work. The holiday photograph is all here: the somewhat apprehensive sitter before a painted backcloth, her companion (perhaps her daughter?) looking on, the children interested in something quite different and the photographer himself under his black hood.

CHILDREN'S CORNER – the beach just south of the spa. As visitors continued to pour into Scarborough all kinds of developments became necessary to cater for their needs and interests. This photograph shows one such improvement. The South Cliff tramway opened in 1875 with the notice which must have relieved many a weary parent: '220 steps avoided for one penny'. And well worth it.

IN COMPLETE CONTRAST to the busy scene above is a deserted slipway and quayside. The only concessions to visitors are two or three bench seats. Note the roofless building on the left – one of the boatyards soon to be demolished in preparation for the development of the harbour area.

AS AT FIRST ERECTED.

THE SPA BRIDGE shown, in the upper drawing, as it was when first erected in 1827. In many ways the developments of modern Scarborough can be said to have started with the building of this bridge. The lower drawing shows it as it was in 1938. The space between the arches of the bridge was filled in by the construction in 1877 of a huge aquarium like those being built at other seaside resorts. This covered about 3 acres and cost £100,000. Its interior architecture was of brick, based on the designs of various Indian palaces and temples. It was later acquired by the Corporation and leased out to various sideshow proprietors and eventually became, ignominiously, a car park.

VALLEY ROAD AS AT PRESENT COVERING AQUARIUM.

THE SPA BRIDGE.

THE ESPLANADE, South Cliff in the early years of the century. '... [We] should like to see,' wrote a newspaper in 1824, 'a Crescent arise of uniform buildings of white stone, elevated on the margin of the cliff ...' It was not until twenty-five years later that the present crescent was begun.

THE CLARENCE GARDENS on the North Bay. These were named after the Duke of Clarence who in 1890 opened the new North Bay promenade, the Royal Albert Drive.

THE MARINE DRIVE. These two photographs show stages in the construction of the Marine Drive, a roadway built round the Castle headland to link the South and North Bays. The foreshore road in the South Bay had been built in 1877 and the Royal Albert Drive in the North Bay was opened in 1890. To link the two was a massive engineering enterprise which if successful would also help to prevent the rapid erosion of the Castle headland. The Corporation borrowed £80,000 to help finance the project and work began in 1897. It was confidently expected that construction would take three years but storms delayed the work which was at last opened in 1908. The first stage of the work was to build a rail causeway on which steam-powered cranes, like the one in the lower photograph, could operate.

THE SWEEP OF THE MARINE DRIVE can be seen on this picture postcard (date stamped 4 August 1913) which also shows Clarence Gardens and Queens Parade.

THE NORTH BAY. Many of the developments of the 1920s and '30s were connected with the North Bay and with the Peasholm area in particular. Peasholm Park itself was opened in 1912. The miniature railway, seen here on the left of the picture, opened in 1930 though its popularity was interrupted by a serious accident the following year.

PEASHOLM PARK, which had been in use since 1912, was extended and extensively developed by the Corporation in 1925. These two photographs show Peasholm Glen before and after this transformation.

CONSTRUCTION OF THE LAKE incorporating an open-air theatre and a miniature railway was a further and most ambitious development. The railway opened in 1931 and the theatre in 1932. The two photographs show the lake under construction. In the centre of the upper photograph is the future stage of the open-air theatre while the lower picture shows the end of the lake and the line of the miniature railway.

A NEW ROAD BRIDGE, seen here under construction (above) and completed (below), was made necessary by the developments in Peasholm. The bridge was opened in 1932.

THE DUCK POND. Scarborough is rich in gardens and ornamental lakes like this one, with its rather unromantic name.

THE PROMENADE PIER, the building of which was an early development in the North Bay. This was 1,000 ft long and supported on cast-iron piles joined by wrought-iron girders. It took three years to build and was opened in 1869. It did not prove profitable and was sold in 1880, the new owners adding a pavilion at the seaward end and shops at its entrance. But it still did not pay and was again sold off cheaply in 1904 before being destroyed by a storm the following year.

THE REMAINS OF THE PIER after the storm of 1905 are shown in these two photographs. The upper picture is of 'Morgan's Island', the pavilion at the seaward end. An effort was made to retain this, especially since it held a liquor licence, but this was unsuccessful and it too was demolished. The lower picture shows the landward end of the pier with its rows of shops. This too was later removed completely. Note the large tented army camp in the background of this picture.

ANOTHER TOURIST ATTRACTION which proved to be a failure was the Warwick Revolving Tower built in 1897 as a 150 ft high viewing platform with a lift. It did not pay and stood disused for years before it was bought by a Mr Shuttleworth – who had it demolished in 1907. Notice the family in the foreground: two at least are more interested in the photographer than the view.

THE GRAND HOTEL which has dominated the Scarborough scene since it was opened in 1867. At the time it was built it was the second largest hotel in Europe. Among the guests who stayed in its early years were the two French poets Rimbaud and Verlaine, and the hotel which figures in the poem 'Promenade' by the former was inspired by the Grand.

ANOTHER VIEW OF THE GRAND HOTEL with a group of idlers looking at a very smart coach and four. Whether this belongs to a guest or to the hotel we do not know.

THE GUESTS of one of the hundreds of boarding houses or small hotels of the town. Though Scarborough's big hotels were much used, the vast majority of visitors stayed in one of these smaller establishments. This group has assembled outside the front door for a photograph. It would be nice to know more about them but we do not even know the name of the house or the date of the picture.

A PROPOSED AMUSEMENT PARK at Scalby Mills. Between the wars there were many plans for the future development of tourism in Scarborough. Some were carried out but others never progressed beyond the first stage. The amusement park was part of an ambitious report prepared for the borough council in 1938 which had to be abandoned the following year on the outbreak of war.

A POSTER first produced in 1915 as a recruiting poster with the slogan 'Remember Scarborough', adapted by the TUC for its conference held in the town in 1925. It urged members to 'Enlist Now – in the ranks of Scarborough's fervent admirers and constant visitors'. As well as a holiday resort Scarborough also became important as a conference centre.

HENRY MAYHEW bought the Theatre Royal in 1888 at a time when, despite having over a century of dramatic performances behind it, the theatre was rapidly losing ground to newer ventures. Mr Mayhew's recipe for reviving it was 'the good old British drama (or melodrama) which if not high art is ... a healthy form of entertainment.'

THE ILL-FATED NORTH PIER, shown here about the turn of the century, made a proper distinction between weekday and Sunday concerts, offering Scarborough's visitors a range of entertainments during their stay.

OUTDOOR ENTERTAINMENT on the beach. Here we see a troupe of pierrots and their audience as well as the usual ice-cream carts and other stalls. In the foreground is a jockey carriage.

A CROWD, with many children, has gathered round this group of beach entertainers at Children's Corner.

THE PUNCH AND JUDY BOOTH on the South Bay, always one of the most popular shows.

A MUZZLED PERFORMING BEAR with its owner on the south shore, an entertainment less acceptable to modern tastes perhaps. The beach strollers here do not seem to be taking much notice of it.

YET ANOTHER BEACH ENTERTAINER is this man with his performing dogs – poodles perhaps. Both he and his assistant are very elaborately dressed.

TOM CARRICK'S ORIGINAL PIERROTS in their traditional costumes and with quite an elaborate stage. They advertise as having 'Royal Patronage', whatever that means. Entertainment troupes like this paid rent to the Corporation for their beach sites. There seems to be a good and appreciative audience.

ANOTHER TROUPE OF PIERROTS on the beach. We cannot see their name unfortunately. The best-known of these troupes was Catlins, whose proprietor, Will Catlin, annoyed by the increasing rent of his beach site, was the first to open an indoor pierrot entertainment at the Arcadia. The usual beach charge was 6d. for a seat, 3d. for standing.

LISTENING TO THE BAND was always an alternative if pierrots were not to your liking – though it must be admitted that there does not seem to be much of an audience at this concert in Clarence Gardens.

SCARBOROUGH'S OPEN-AIR THEATRE in its lake setting has been a tremendous attraction since its opening in 1932, lending itself to large and spectacular sets like the one shown here, which was used in the very popular (if rather jingoist) *Merrie England*. Below are some of the cast looking pleased with themselves, as indeed they had a perfect right to be!

COMPANIES OF MINSTRELS, with their tambourines, extravagant make-up and 'plantation' songs, were perhaps even more popular than the pierrots. This photograph is unfortunately not dated.

SCARBOROUGH in the 1920s and '30s could certainly provide a wide choice of theatrical entertainment. This is Richard Jerome's 'Rolling Stones' party, who performed at the Floral Hall, which opened in 1910 and specialized in these 'spectacular' shows, in 1934.

TWO TABLEAUX FROM THE SHOW. Above 'A Greek Frieze' and below 'Autumn'.

AT THE ARCADE
WEDNESDAY TO SATURDAY
FEB. 7TH. 8TH. 9TH. & 10TH. AT 7-45 P.M.
SATURDAY MATINEE AT 2 P.M.

"HOBSON'S CHOICE,"
A DIALECT COMEDY.

BOX OFFICE NOW OPEN AT ARCHIBALD RAMSDENS
HUNTRISS ROW.
IN AID OF THE SCARBORO' DISTRICT NURSING ASS'.
AND THE LEAGUE OF HELP.

A WORLD-FAMOUS ACTOR who never forgot his early connections with Scarborough was Charles Laughton, whose brother Tom was for many years the owner of the Pavilion Hotel. This showcard advertises the Scarborough amateur players' production of *Hobson's Choice* at the Arcade in 1923 with Charles Laughton and Mrs Rowntree in the leading roles.

MOST PEOPLE WILL REMEMBER Laughton's film performance as Hobson, the drunken autocratic father, but in the 1923 production he played Willy Mossop, the journeyman cobbler who married his employer's daughter. This was the role played in the film by John Mills. On the first night of the play the theatre was almost empty but was soon playing to full houses. The *Scarborough Mercury* wrote of Charles Laughton's performance '... ranking with the best examples of character portrayal ... Mr Laughton's study of the evolution of the dullard was a splendid effort of the actor's art ...'

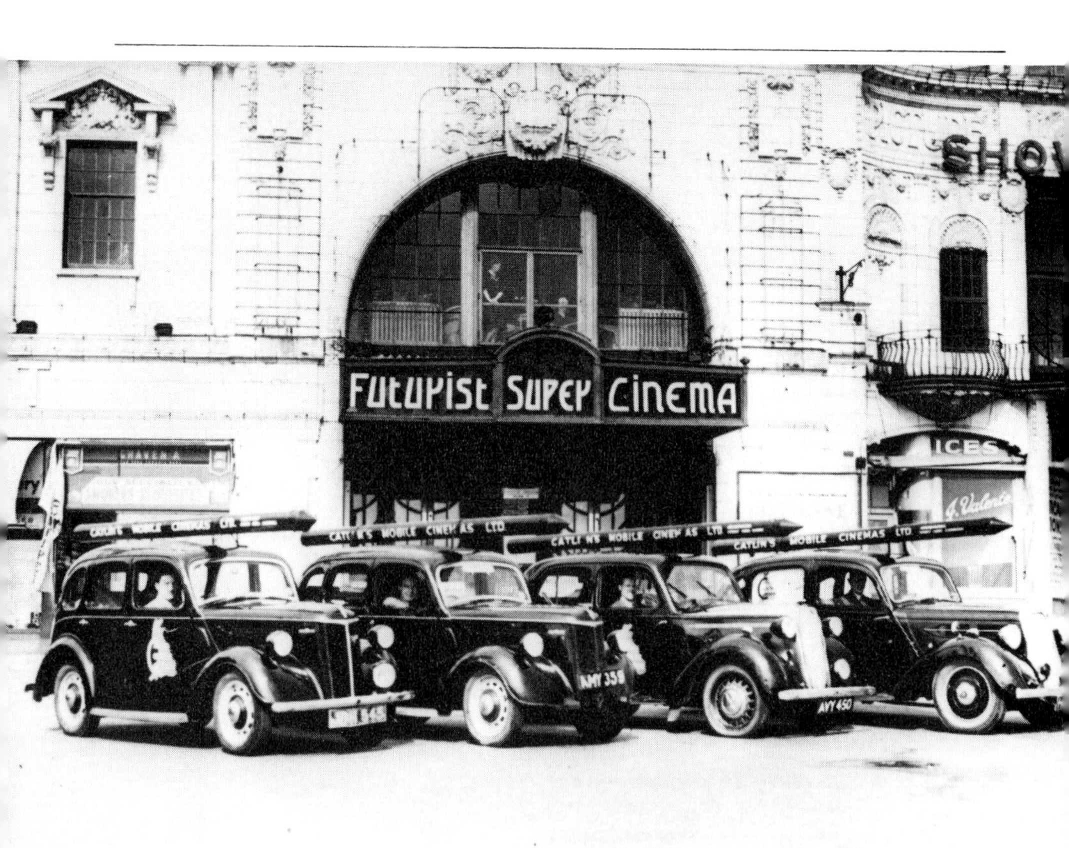

CINEMAS TOO FLOURISHED in the town; the North Bay cinema was paying patrons' tramfares in 1918, the Aberdeen Walk opened in 1920, the Futurist in 1921, the Capitol in 1929 and the Odeon in 1936. In the 1930s Catlins also operated a mobile cinema service for the town. A screen is attached to the roof of each of the four cars shown here outside the Futurist.

SIGHT-SEEING WAS ALSO AN IMPORTANT PART of a Scarborough holiday. Here on the Esplanade a family is setting off in a very smart coach and four. Father is standing rather importantly facing the camera while the rest of the family including, one suspects, a governess are on top where they can get a good view of the countryside.

THE ADVANTAGES OF THE JOCKEY-CARRIAGE seen in this picture with three lady passengers, was that the occupants were not incommoded by the presence of a driver, who rode rather than drove the horse.

CHAS. GADDY'S Noted Four-Horse Chars-a-banc.

. . . . "THE VIVID," . . . .

The Smartest Turnout in Scarborough, leaves the GRAND HOTEL for the Principal Drives at 10-30 A.M. and 2-30P.M.

Special Terms to Private Parties. Mews at the Back of Albermarle Crescent.

THE EARLY CHARABANCS were horse-drawn vehicles like this one of Charles Gaddy's, advertised as 'the smartest turn-out in Scarborough'. Ward Lock's *Guide* of 1911 informs visitors that '. . . chars-a-banc and waggonettes run daily to Forge Valley, Hackness, Silpho Moor, Hayburn Wyke and Filey . . . usual fare 2 shillings . . . the N.E. Railway Co. also maintains a fleet of motor chars-a-banc . . .'

THE PADDLE-STEAMER *COMET* leaving harbour with a full load of sight-seeing passengers. When not engaged in fishing it was usual for boats to take visitors on short sea trips. Theakston's *Guide*, 1880, recommended '. . . a run out to sea and back again . . . in a steamboat . . . there need be no fear as to the safety of any of the vessels . . . the steamers are all subjected to periodical official inspection and they are also limited as to the number of passengers each shall carry . . .' Paddle-steamers like this were in use at Scarborough between about 1880 and 1910.

THE ESSENTIAL PART OF A HOLIDAY, for many, was to be able to sit in the sun and watch the world go by, or simply sit, or sleep – despite all the activities available to the holidaymaker. The building in the background of this photograph was the Rowing Clubhouse.

A RATHER DIFFERENT TOURIST. Quite where this holidaymaker came from is difficult to say. The swan seems more interested in finding out its weight than in the Angling Festival of September 1931.

A GROUP OF CHILDREN for whom a trip to see Mr George Royle's 'Imps', either on the South Sands or in the Floral Hall, seems unlikely. Entertainment was primarily for visitors rather than residents. This is a lovely photograph of childhood, carefully composed with contrasts of light and of shade. Unfortunately we do not know who the photographer was.

SECTION THREE

The Port

THE HARBOUR

THE HARBOUR AT SCARBOROUGH. The history of this harbour can be said to begin with a grant of duties for five years by Henry III in 1252. 'To make certain new port with timber and stone towards the sea whereby all ships arriving there may enter and sail out without danger . . . ye may take in the said port of every merchants ship sixpence . . . of every fishermans ship fourpence . . . and of every fishermans boat twopence . . .' The story of the harbour since then is long and complex, punctuated by storms, damage, rebuilding and usually shortage of money.

KING RICHARD III HOUSE. Even before 1252 there was a fishing village under the Castle cliff and building continued to take place up the cliff side and even on the sand. One or two of the medieval houses remain including this, known as King Richard III House. At the time of this photograph it housed the Missions to Seamen.

THE CORNER OF SANDSIDE AND THE LIGHTHOUSE PIER with a group of idlers leaning against the wall. The steps on the right led to the old Watch House which was accidentally burnt down. An old tar barrel used to be placed here which was set on fire in bad weather to warn ships not to enter the harbour.

A PEACEFUL SCENE IN THE SLIPWAY. Two men – Mr Lancaster and Mr Anderson – are seated on ships' masts. A coble is drawn up at the head of the slipway. Behind is Sandside with the Lancaster Inn on the left and in the background the Castle walls with the old barrack building clearly visible. The photograph is undated but is certainly pre-1914.

SAILING COBLES in the harbour. Again, an undated photograph but certainly pre-1914.

AN EARLY PHOTOGRAPH of the harbour with cobles loaded with barrels plying between the fishing fleet and the shore, watched by children on the beach. Note the two remarkable perambulators.

A LIGHTHOUSE was in existence early in the nineteenth century according to Hinderwell's *History of Scarborough* but there seems to have been a number of alterations and after the bombardment of 1914 it was largely rebuilt. Strangely little detail of the history of the lighthouse is available.

THE OUTER HARBOUR with sailing yards and a paddle-steamer. Though the harbour was allowed to be the only real place of refuge between Tyne and Humber, it had many real disadvantages, suffering from the accumulation of sand banks. According to Hinderwell's *History of Scarborough,* until the New Pier was built at the beginning of the nineteenth century the harbour was 'truly dangerous' and 'not much superior to the open shore'. In later times its chief disadvantage for sailing ships wishing to use it during a storm was that it was often full of moored fishing vessels leaving no room for emergencies.

THE HARBOUR AND THE OLD PIER shown in an unusually clear and accomplished early photograph. The picture is full of detail and merits close study. Unfortunately it is not dated but certainly pre-dates the construction of the Marine Drive at around the turn of the century.

HORSES AND CARTS are leading away loads of gravel which had been brought in by coble from Cayton Bay, probably for use in building the Marine Drive.

CEMENT BEING UNLOADED from a ship at the lighthouse pier for the same building project.

SAILING DRIFTERS in the harbour. A report by the harbour commissioners in 1942 pointed out that '. . . this port has always been a fishing port and what other trade it has enjoyed has been accidental and spasmodical . . .' During the fourteenth century, however, Scarborough had had a near monopoly of trade with Iceland, but by 1436 a poet could write of how from Bristol ships had to Iceland '. . . gone and come as men were wont of old of Scarborough onto the costes cold . . .'

A DREDGER on loan from the British Dredging Co. from Southampton. Because the harbour is tidal it has always been subject to silting and since about 1880 has had to be dredged at frequent intervals. Since the port did not have its own dredger one had to be hired.

FIVE FISHERMEN outside the Bell Hotel on Bland's Cliff. They are not wearing their sea-boots but have donned their sou'westers, presumably for the benefit of the photographer.

THE FISHING INDUSTRY was of primary importance to Scarborough, as is shown by the fact that it was chosen as the theme for this New Year card in 1902–3. Theakston's *Guide* of 1880 says '. . . fish in Scarborough is generally abundant and of the best quality: cod, ling, halibut, turbot, skate, codling, haddock, whiting, mackerel, sole, dab, plaice, herring, gurnard, coalfish, lobster, crab, shrimp etc . . .' It was, however, the herring fishery which was of the greatest importance during its short season.

PART OF THE FISHING FLEET in the South Bay, more ships in the harbour, cobles lying off the beach, and all sorts of activities going on on the foreshore make this a fascinating and marvellously detailed photograph. During the herring season Scarborough was visited by drifters from the other herring fishing ports from Scotland to Cornwall. In 1896 two gunboats were stationed in the bay in case of trouble between fishermen from Lowestoft and Cornwall.

LINE FISHING STARTS HERE: digging for bait on the sands.

A GROUP OF FISHERMEN – and of course a dog – on Sandgale corner with Eastbrough in the background.

THE NORTH WHARF, Sandside. Herrings are being unloaded from a boat and tipped into tubs.

THE HERRING SALE. Herring fishermen brought samples of their catch for sale. The measure used was the 'cran' of four baskets or about one thousand fish. As late as 1929, no less than 11,300 crans were landed during the two months of August and September. The best fish went to the home and London markets with the rest exported or sent for curing.

FISH STALLS on the south side. The lifeboat house can be seen centre right.

THE FISH MARKET, before the fish pier was widened. Notice the dangerously narrow path between the stalls and the harbour! Fish were auctioned here and the auction was always begun by the ringing of a bell.

FISH (HERRING) PACKING at the East Pier end. There seem to be more watchers than workers in this picture.

FISHER GIRLS AT WORK. During the herring season the migrating fish were followed south along the coast by the drifters. Following the fishing fleet were the fisher girls, mostly Scots, who gutted, sorted and packed the herring. They worked very quickly – supposedly gutting fifty fish a minute – sorted the fish by eye into six different sizes, and packed them in barrels.

ANOTHER GROUP AT WORK on the West Pier. Some idea of the vast numbers of fish landed can be gained from the stacks of barrels ready to receive them. The herring fishery declined dramatically during the 1930s partly because shoals of fish were fewer and smaller and partly because fishing was closely regulated. New regulations meant that Scarborough was not included in the fishing ports.

TWO FISHER GIRLS rolling a barrel of herring along the quayside. Before the First World War many barrels of herring were exported to Russia. After the war most of the sailing drifters like those seen here had been replaced by steamers.

SUCCESSFUL FISHERMEN with their catches. For a few years it seemed as if Scarborough would become the centre of a new fishing industry: game fishing with rod and line for tunny. The first of these huge fish was landed in 1930 and the British Tunny Club with its headquarters at Scarborough was founded in 1932. Until the war, which put a stop to it, the sport was highly successful. After the war it revived but few fish were caught, the last three being hooked in 1954.

SCARBOROUGH'S SHIPBUILDING INDUSTRY was certainly in existence during the thirteenth century and continued to be a significant factor in the town's economy for the next six hundred years. Even after the last yard – Tindalls – closed in 1867 boats continued to be built and a directory of 1892 lists three boat-builders. The construction of the Marine Drive (begun in 1897) swept away the remains of the old shipyards. This picture is undated but must have been taken before work began on the new road.

SHIPYARDS AND THE HARBOUR in around 1860. Hinderwell's *History of Scarborough* gives an average of nine ships per year – most of them small – being built at the end of the eighteenth century. The Napoleonic Wars led to a brief period of prosperity but after 1820 decline was rapid. In this interesting photograph one ship is being built on a cradle (centre right) and others are in various stages of completion. A steam paddle tug is tied up (left) and large mooring buoys dot the harbour. The island pier (centre) was removed in 1880.

THE CHANGING FACE OF THE HARBOUR. Although many of the buildings seen in the preceeding photograph are still there, the harbour has changed: the island pier has been replaced and no ships are being built, though it looks as though one or two may be being repaired. The skyline too has changed, being dominated by the Grand Hotel.

SAILING YAWLS in the inner harbour, and a small ferry coble.

THE YAWL was used both for line fishing and drift netting. The upper picture shows a single yawl with the Grand Hotel in the background. In the lower picture is a group of yawls in the South Bay. An article in the *Scarborough Gazette* – quoted in Theakston's *Guide* of 1880 – dealt with the fishing industry and described the boats: '. . . the boats commonly used . . . are the yawl and the coble. The former are decked boats . . . the value of a yawl is about £500 . . .'

A HERRING DRIFTER with a steam-powered winch. Her name cannot be seen but she was a St Ives boat – a long way from home. In the background are several cobles of different sizes. The *Scarborough Mercury* described the coble as '. . . about 27 feet long . . . used to advantage when the herring lie near the shore . . . the value of a coble is £50–£70 . . .'

THE STEAM PADDLE TUG *ALEXANDRA* towing boats into harbour. During the great storm of 1880 she attempted without success to tow to safety ships in distress. The tall arches of the Spa Bridge can be seen in the background but perhaps the Aquarium had not yet been built beneath them.

SCARBOROUGH'S PADDLE-STEAMERS in action. Around the turn of the century Scarborough, unlike most other fishing ports, had a small fleet of steamers which often combined two functions: when not wanted for fishing the boat would carry passengers. The upper picture shows an unnamed paddle boat entering the harbour. The lower shows the paddle-steamer *Cambria* leaving harbour. The *Cambria* went ashore at Gristhorpe in 1912.

TWO PADDLE-STEAMERS berthed at the lighthouse pier. These boats usually fished fairly close to the shore for short periods rather than going well out to sea and staying there for several weeks as did the sailing trawlers. Occasionally, however, they did venture further, even as far as Icelandic waters. Their safety record was not very good. The boat on the left, the *Lord Clyde,* was run down and sunk in 1893.

TWO MORE PADDLE TRAWLERS berthed side by side. The outer one was the *Constance,* an iron vessel of 91 tons, built in 1882. She was the last of the Scarborough paddle trawlers and was wrecked at Hartlepool in 1910.

A LOVELY PICTURE of a Scarborough coble with mudlarks playing round her and ships' masts at the bottom of the slipway.

A FISHING SMACK is firmly aground in this undated photograph. Sudden easterly gales often resulted in sailing ships suffering the same fate in the South Bay, especially if the harbour was crowded. The children seem to have lost interest but the group of men gathered round are probably debating the chances of floating her off.

AN UNNAMED THREE-MASTER also aground in the South Bay.

THE WRECK OF THE *MARY*, driven ashore on 26 October 1869. A dramatic eyewitness account of the rescue of the crew by rocket apparatus and breeches buoy is given in Rowntree's *History of Scarborough*.

THE WRECK OF THE *LILY*. One of the most destructive storms to hit Scarborough was that of October 1880 when many ships sought shelter in the harbour or were driven ashore. Again, there is a full eyewitness account of the rescue operations in Rowntree's *History of Scarborough*. This is the wreck of the *Lily*: '. . . I never saw such a sad sight . . . everybody gave her up for lost but the rocket apparatus was despatched . . . the seventh rocket took effect and they got the men ashore . . .'

ANOTHER VICTIM of the same storm was this vessel, the *5 Gebrüder*.

THE *GASTRY* (OR *GLASTRY*) OF MARYPORT with the crowded harbour in the background make this a dramatic picture.

THE *BOSPHORUS,* yet another casualty of the storm of 1880!

THE SCHOONER *SATELLITE,* blown ashore in 1901, was one of the many other wrecks caused by many other storms.

THE LIFEBOAT shown here on its carriage ready for launching was the *Lady Leigh*, which was given to Scarborough by the Freemasons of Warwickshire. She was on station from 1872 to 1887, being launched 42 times and helping to save 106 lives. The town was one of the first ports to have a regular lifeboat, one being stationed there as early as 1800.

THE LIFEBOAT *QUEENSBURY* on its carriage with crew all in place. The little crowd of boys are enjoying having their photographs taken but they have been carefully posed by the photographer for this is obviously an official occasion, perhaps the handing over of a new boat. Scarborough had three boats named *Queensbury* and it is not certain which of the three is pictured here.

THE *QUEENSBURY* AT PRACTICE in the harbour mouth. The rowers on one side pulled blue oars, on the other, white. Regular practice was necessary if the lifeboat was to be efficiently manned.

LAUNCHING THE LIFEBOAT.

THE LIFEBOAT IN ACTION. It is difficult to tell from this picture whether the boat is being launched or is returning. Since the crowds are running towards the sea it is probably the former.

THE LIFEBOAT *QUEENSBURY III* RIDING A BIG WAVE. She was on station from 1902 to 1918, was launched 60 times and helped to save 98 lives.

THE *HERBERT JOY,* Scarborough's first motor lifeboat, presented by Mr Alex Joy in 1923 in memory of his brother who had been drowned in the bay.

THE COXSWAIN of the Scarborough lifeboat, Mr John Owston (left), with the medal which he was awarded for gallantry after the 1880 storm. With him is the second coxswain Mr Claybourne.

SECTION FOUR

People and Events

PEOPLE

THE PRINCE OF WALES (later King Edward VII), one of the many eminent visitors to Scarborough, who stayed with the Earl of Londesborough in 1869, '70 and '71.

LORD LONDESBOROUGH, one of the principal landowners of Scarborough, was among the leading citizens of the borough featured in a series of articles published by the *Scarborough Magazine* at the turn of the century. Apart from his interest in farming and especially horse-breeding, he is remembered for instituting the Scarborough Cricket Festival. His title is commemorated in several Scarborough streets and buildings.

SIR GEORGE SITWELL. Though the seat of the Sitwell family was Renishaw in Derbyshire, their connection with Scarborough began in the early eighteenth century. Sir George spent his early years there and after his marriage to the daughter of Lord Londesborough spent much of each year there. In 1885 he was elected MP (Conservative). The *Scarborough Mercury* (Liberal) alleged that his election '... was secured by means which we trust the Liberals of the borough will never degrade themselves by resorting to ...' It also pointed out that joining the Conservative party was likely to lead to '... deviation from the path of sobriety ... progress on the downward path which has led to bankruptcy, ruin and disgrace ...' The best accounts of Sir George's eccentric life are to be found in the writings of his famous children, Osbert, Sacheverell and Edith.

SIR FREDERICK (LATER LORD) LEIGHTON was born in Scarborough though most of his early life was spent abroad. From about 1855 he became an immensely popular artist and was elected President of the Royal Academy in 1878. On this occasion he was presented with an illuminated address by the artist community of the town.

EDWIN BROUGH JP came to live in Scarborough in 1882. Here he began to breed bloodhounds, becoming perhaps the most successful breeder of his day in the world. His hounds are best remembered not for this success but for a failure: at the request of the police Mr Brough took two of his hounds to London in an attempt to trace Jack the Ripper.

DAVID HUNTER was the youngest of five cricketing brothers. In 1888 he succeeded his elder brother as regular wicket-keeper for Yorkshire, a position which he held for many years.

FISHERMEN MATTHEW BULLAMORE AND HIS SON MYER who is repairing a lobster pot – citizens who are just as representative of Scarborough life even though not interviewed by the *Scarborough Magazine*.

MR JOHN OWSTON SENIOR, the most notable of Scarborough lifeboatmen. He served as coxswain for 41 years during which time the lifeboat saved 230 lives. He retired in 1912 and was succeeded by his son, also John.

'PLATTY' GOTH, a shellfish hawker, photographed with his basket and shrimp net in about 1890.

MR LANCASTER, the skipper of a fishing yawl, walking across from his home in a tenement block in Sandside, *c.* 1905.

MR HENRY W. SMITH was borough engineer from 1897 to 1931. He was responsible for designing and carrying out many of the tourist developments in Scarborough and especially for the Peasholm projects. He is seen here in his office on the day of his retirement.

THE VICAR OF ST SAVIOUR'S selling religious tracts in Aberdeen Walk.

AN ANONYMOUS FISHERGIRL – even the date of the photograph is not known. There are very many photographs of people whose identity has been long forgotten but whose pictures are no less important and interesting for that.

A FAMILY GROUP outside the Scalby Mills Hotel. The little girl on horseback seems happy enough but her brother (?) holding the reins seems a little apprehensive. We do not know who they are or the date of the photograph.

A FINE PORTRAIT of a young man with a barrel organ. These itinerant street musicians were very much a part of Scarborough life during the season.

A PONY-DRAWN BARREL ORGAN or hurdy-gurdy. In the first volume of his autobiography, Sir Osbert Sitwell, who was born in 1892, records hearing the hurdy-gurdy under his nursery window in Scarborough and remembered being allowed to throw down two or three pennies wrapped in paper to the proprietor.

ANOTHER ANONYMOUS CHARACTER is this bearded man leaning on a barrel in the brewery yard of G. & H. Hudson, brewers, maltsters, spirit merchants, North Street Brewery, Scarborough. This is a detail of the photograph on page 36.

A GROUP OF LOCALS interrupted in their gossip and knitting to pose – rather ungraciously? – for their photographs.

TWO SCOTS FISHERGIRLS chatting to a seaman on the quay – a much more cheerful group, probably because it was not posed.

A HISTORIC EVENT: one of the first airmen to visit the town was W.C. Hucks, seen here flying over the herring fleet in the South Bay in 1912. It must have been difficult for the photographer to catch an aeroplane in flight and as we can see he has only just succeeded.

THE OPENING OF THE VALLEY BRIDGE. Communications between the town and the South Cliff had always been difficult because of the deep gorge occupied by the Plantation. In 1862 one Robert Williamson, who was interested in developing the largely unoccupied South Cliff, bought an iron bridge which had collapsed into the River Ouse at York. The Corporation decided to support his venture and the bridge was brought to Scarborough, re-erected and opened in 1865 as a toll bridge. This picture shows a procession crossing the new Valley Bridge to mark its opening. The bridge was 800 ft long and 80 ft high. The toll charged was one halfpenny per person.

THE OPENING CEREMONY of the new Valley Bridge. As the twentieth century advanced and traffic increased it became obvious that the Valley Bridge did not have the capacity which was needed. It was freed from toll in 1919, thus speeding up traffic flow, but a new and wider bridge was eventually built and opened in 1928.

THE AMBITIOUS MARINE DRIVE PROJECT has been mentioned in earlier pages. This photograph shows the laying of the last block on 1 October 1904. The project had cost £105,000, £28,000 more than had been estimated. Though it was virtually completed in 1904 after seven years' work, extensive storm damage in 1905 and 1906 meant that it was not opened until 1908.

THE CIVIC DIGNITARIES of the town assembled before the statue of Queen Victoria to hear the proclamation of the accession of George V in 1910.

ANOTHER OFFICIAL OCCASION. The coronation of Edward VII and Alexandra was marked by a procession seen here moving along Westborough.

A PROCESSION which seems to be somewhat later in date but so far I have not been able to identify the occasion.

THE YORK DISTRICT SYNOD of 1897. Scarborough has over the years played host to many conferences, many of which were commemorated by formal group photographs. Few, however, can have been as impressive as this, when about 140 members and friends were taken for a drive round Forge Valley and Hackness.

OFFICIAL VISITORS OF A DIFFERENT KIND are shown here when the Channel Fleet visited Scarborough in 1908. The top picture shows the battleship *Royal Sovereign* while, below, the pleasure boat *White Lady* takes passengers out to the battleship *Hood*.

TWO MORE ROYAL NAVY VISITS are illustrated by these pictures. Above, the mayor is seated with the crew of HM drifter *Leeward* in 1934. Below, the mayor and other visitors are welcomed aboard HMS *Malaya.*

QUEEN MARIE OF ROMANIA visits the miniature railway in 1934.

THE MAYOR, MR PINDAR, welcomes delegates to the NUM national conference in 1932. On Mr Pindar's right is the miners' leader Peter Lee.

THE OPENING OF THE NALGO HOLIDAY CAMP at Cayton Bay, c. 1930.

THE YORKSHIRE DIALECT SOCIETY'S VISIT in 1936. Conferences were not always large affairs with many guests.

SCARBOROUGH'S SUBMARINE WEEK. One cannot help but admire the ingenuity which went into the production of this realistic float seen outside the Pavilion Hotel during Scarborough's 'submarine week' in 1919. Instead of the conventional U-number this U-boat is labelled 'U-do your bit'!

AN ENTIRELY UNOFFICIAL OCCASION: a local band in fancy dress. The occasion and the date are unknown but the fun and high spirits are unmistakable.

AN IMPORTANT EVENT FOR THOSE CONCERNED, although here again the date and occasion are forgotten. A small display has been erected in a corner of the Spa ballroom and a group of all ages and both sexes is posed before it. Was it political? or religious? and what was the organization? These are tantalizing questions.

IN CONTRAST, we do know what these occasions were and when they took place. In the upper picture the staff of Boyes stores are setting off on their annual outing in 1914. They went to Kirkbymoorside. Below, a church choir is also off on an annual trip. This was in 1927 and they went to Rievaulx Abbey.

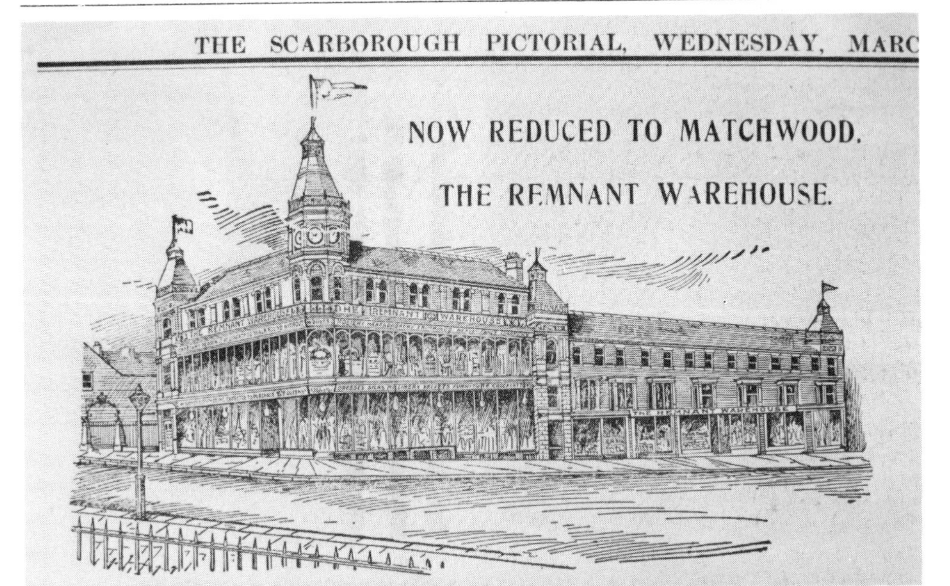

THE SCARBOROUGH PICTORIAL, WEDNESDAY, MARC

NOW REDUCED TO MATCHWOOD.

THE REMNANT WAREHOUSE.

BOYES REMNANT WAREHOUSE, destroyed by fire in 1915. Scarborough had its share of less pleasant events also. These two illustrations from the *Scarborough Pictorial* of 3 March 1915 show Boyes Remnant Warehouse before and after the fire which gutted many of the premises in Queen Street. Fortunately there were no casualties.

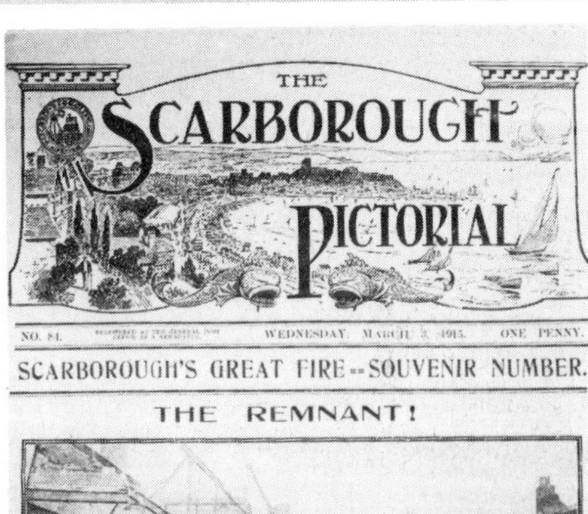

THE SCARBOROUGH PICTORIAL

NO. 84. WEDNESDAY, MARCH 3, 1915. ONE PENNY.

SCARBOROUGH'S GREAT FIRE—SOUVENIR NUMBER.

THE REMNANT!

A SPECTACULAR ACCIDENT in September 1925 but, again, fortunately no one was killed. A tram left the rails and went through the roof of the old Aquarium ballroom. The driver, a Mr Richardson, stayed at the controls and suffered only minor injuries, as did the few passengers who had jumped to safety.

THE DESTRUCTION OF THE NORTH BAY PIER by a gale in 1905 has already been described. This picture shows how complete the destruction was.

THE FIRST WORLD WAR takes its toll. Shortly after the beginning of the war the mayor of Scarborough, in an article for the *Scarborough Mercury,* attacked 'foolish and baseless rumours' such as that the town might be attacked from the sea, which were causing holiday makers to leave. On 16 December 1914, however, German battleships opened fire on the town. The attack lasted some forty-five minutes, a great deal of damage was done and nineteen people were killed. The upper picture shows the shop of Joseph Merryweather whose wife was killed as she tried to help customers to safety. In the lower picture we can see the damage done to the barracks on Castle Hill.

A MORE FAMILIAR THREAT, the sea presented much more regular incidents. This dramatic photograph shows crowds gathered round a ship stranded on the sands of the South Bay.

THE CAST OF *HIAWATHA,* an open-air theatre production, meet the mayor, mayoress and other Corporation officials on a much more cheerful occasion.

SCARBOROUGH'S CONTINUING HISTORY. With the exception of the last two, all the photographs in this book date from before the Second World War. These are included as a reminder that the story of Scarborough goes on and that the earlier photographs must be looked at in the context of later events. The end of the Second World War was marked by a Thanksgiving Week in the town when, among other events, this Spitfire was placed on view.

A MEMORIAL STATUE of Sir George Cayley (1773–1857), a local landowner, who was the inventor of the first flying model helicopter and one of the great pioneers of aeronautics. This final photograph provides a link with Scarborough as it was in the days before photography. It shows a ceremony held to mark the centenary of the death of this, one of Scarborough's most remarkable citizens.

ACKNOWLEDGEMENTS

Laurence Sterne, a regular visitor to Scarborough, asked in his inimitable book *Tristram Shandy*, '... shall we for ever make new books, as apothecaries make new mixtures, by pouring out of one vessel into another?'

I have tried, so far as I have been able, to avoid this by using photographs which have not appeared elsewhere or have at least been little used. There are however exceptions and the reader may find some pictures familiar.

My particular thanks are due to my brother-in-law and sister Dr and Mrs R. Zissler and their many friends in Scarborough without whom this book would not have been possible.

Photographs have been lent and help has been given by the following, to whom I wish to express my sincere thanks:

Mrs J. Bayse • Mr T. Pinder • Mr P. Boyes • Mr C.G. Rhodes • Mrs Coopland
Scarborough Public Library • Mr J. Crawford •Mr Swalwell • Mrs Hardisty
Mr K. Taylor • Mrs Jenkinson • Mr G.G. Walker • Mrs Milne • Mr M.C. Wheeler
Mrs D. Pashby • Mr A. Wray

I am also grateful to Mr P. Boyes for allowing me to use photographs from the collection of the late Mr E. Hopwood.

Any errors in the book, whether of omission or commission, remain the responsibility of the author.